How To Use This Book

Example: G Major Scale

Sample A: G_____D_____A_____E_____

Sample B: 0 1 2 3   0 1 2 3   0 1 2 3   0 1 2

Beginners: How to read instructional notation.

Sample A= tells you which string to play on
Sample B= tells you which finger to use on that string

1= index finger- place on the marker closest to the scroll
2= middle finger- place on middle marker
3= ring finger- place on marker closest to you

NOTE: In the scale above, the 2nd finger on both the A string and E string should be placed between the first and second markers. (1st and 2nd fingers touching)

I have used this method with my beginner students for years and it has been incredibly successful. Many students will be playing within hours due to this form of fiddle tablature.

Each fiddle tune has 2 versions on facing pages: a beginner version with fiddle tablature and a more challenging version with notation and guitar chords for accompaniment.
Both versions are on facing pages so that a beginner reading the left page can be accompanied by a guitarist with guitar chords readily available on the right page.

How to Hold Your Fiddle

You should place your fiddle on your left shoulder against your neck. Then tilt your head towards the fiddle and cradle it between your jaw and neck. Allow your jaw to rest on the chin rest.

<u>Pointers:</u>

You want your fiddle to feel like an extension of your body. It should be level to the ground. Use a mirror to make sure your fiddle is level.

**An easy way to remember this is to avoid ski slopes by pointing the scroll up and try to avoid sledding hills by pointing the scroll down towards the ground. Keep it level!

Use the picture below as a guide.

CELTIC FIDDLING
MADE EASY

20 FAVORITE CELTIC TUNES, IN BEGINNING AND INTERMEDIATE VERSIONS

ARRANGED AND EDITED BY CARRIE L. STUCKERT

Online Audio   www.melbay.com/21442BCDEB

Audio contents

1	Tuning	12	After the Battle of Aughrim
2	The Road to Lisdoonvarna	13	Bonaparte
3	Ye Banks and Braes	14	Star of the County Down
4	The Parting Glass	15	Itchy Fingers
5	Red is the Rose	16	Londonderry Air or Danny Boy
6	Scarborough Fair	17	Ballydesmond Polka Set
7	May the Road Rise to Meet You	18	Swallow Tail's Jig
8	MacPherson's Farewell	19	The Irish Washerwoman
9	Wild Mountain Thyme	20	The Morning Dew
10	Erin's Green Shore	21	Banish Misfortune
11	The Salley Gardens		

Recorded at Stage 1 Productions
Fiddle: Carrie L. Stuckert • Guitar: David A. Hanson

1 2 3 4 5 6 7 8 9 0

Visit us on the Web at www.melbay.com — E-mail us at email@melbay.com

Table of Contents

How to Hold Your Bow

The easiest way to learn a good bow hold is to make a rabbit with your right hand. Place your two middle fingers together and put them over your thumb while keeping your index and pinky fingers curved. Make sure all your fingers are curved. Use the picture below as a guide.

Once you have a rabbit made with your hand, set it on your bow. Your thumb should be placed touching both the stick and frog, your two middle fingers stay together and go over the top, while your index and pinky fingers stay curved and rest on the top of the bow. Use the pictures below as a guide.

Bow hold prep: Rabbit

Bow hold: Place Rabbit on Bow

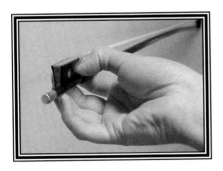

Thumb placement on Bow

Tuning Your Fiddle

A fiddle is tuned to perfect fifths which means that there are 5 pitches or notes in between each string.

Tuning with a piano:

A piano may be used to tune your fiddle. Middle C is the 4th set of twin black keys from the right on a piano. The diagram below is not a full keyboard; however, it shows the keys to use to tune your strings.

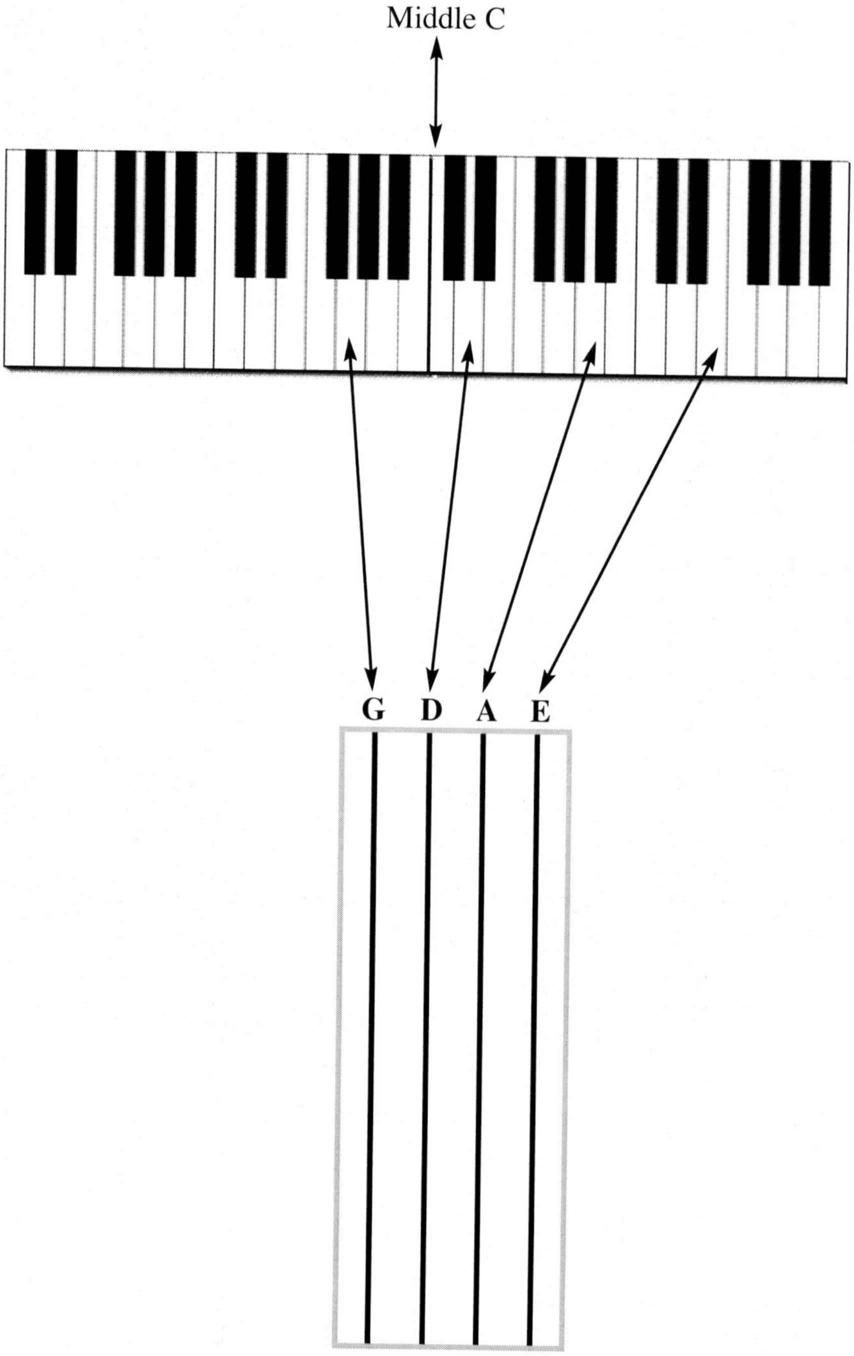

Middle C

Tuning with a tuner:
Tuning with an electronic tuner is the most accurate method of tuning your fiddle. There are several models to choose from.

G D A E

Tuning using the CD:
A tuning sample is provided on the CD; match your pitch to the CD to tune your fiddle.

Putting Tapes or Stickers on Your Fiddle

Small round stickers or tape strips can be used to mark your finger placement on the fingerboard. These act as a guide so you know where to place your fingers. Fretted instruments such as guitars have frets to show you where to put your fingers. Fiddle players have to learn where to put their fingers. **These markers will act as a guide to help you play your fiddle in tune.**

Instructions:

1. Make sure your fiddle is in tune.
2. On the "A" string find the pitch that matches your "D" string and mark where your finger is with a pencil. This is where you will place your marker to mark your third finger (ring finger) placement. This should measure approximately 3 1/4" from the nut (top of fingerboard).
3. On the "D" string find the pitch that matches your "E" string and mark where your finger is with a pencil. This is where you will place your marker to mark your first finger (index finger) placement. This should measure approximately 1 1/4" from the nut.
4. The final marker you place is for your second finger (middle finger) which is placed in between the first and third finger markers measuring approximately 2 1/2" from the nut.

**Use the picture below as a guideline for sticker/tape placement.

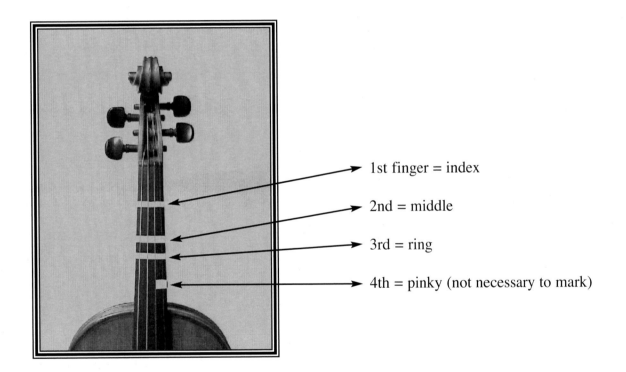

1st finger = index

2nd = middle

3rd = ring

4th = pinky (not necessary to mark)

The Road to Lisdoonvarna

Beginner Fingerings

Traditional Irish

Note: The second finger on the E string should
be placed between the 1st and 2nd markers.
(1st and 2nd fingers touch)

© Arranged and Edited by Carrie L. Stuckert 2005

The Road to Lisdoonvarna

Intermediate
with Guitar Chords

Traditional Irish

Ye Banks and Braes

Beginner Fingerings

Traditional Scottish

Note: (/) is a slide which means you place your finger
a half step below the pitch and slide up to the notated pitch.
Slides are located in measures: 8 and 22.

© Arranged and Edited by Carrie L. Stuckert 2005

Ye Banks and Braes

Intermediate
with Guitar Chords

Traditional Scottish

The Parting Glass

Beginner Fingerings

Traditional Irish

Note: The second finger on the E string should
be placed between the 1st and 2nd markers.
(1st and 2nd fingers touch)

© Arranged and Edited by Carrie L. Stuckert 2005

12

The Parting Glass

Intermediate
with Guitar Chords

Traditional Irish

Red is the Rose

Beginner Fingerings

Traditional Irish

Note: The second finger on the E string should be placed between the 1st and 2nd markers. (1st and 2nd fingers touch)

© Arranged and Edited by Carrie L. Stuckert 2005

Red is the Rose

Intermediate
with Guitar Chords

Traditional Irish

© Arranged and Edited by Carrie L. Stuckert 2005

Scarborough Fair

Beginner Fingerings

Traditional Scottish

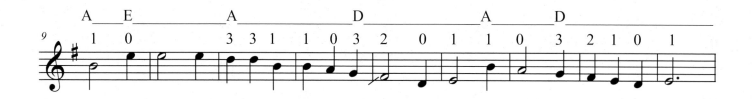

© Arranged and Edited by Carrie L. Stuckert 2005

Scarborough Fair

Intermediate
with Guitar Chords

Traditional Scottish

© Arranged and Edited by Carrie L. Stuckert 2005

May The Road Rise to Meet You

Beginner Fingerings

Traditional Irish

Note: The second finger on the E string should
be placed between the 1st and 2nd markers.
(1st and 2nd fingers touch)

© Arranged and Edited by Carrie L. Stuckert 2005

May The Road Rise to Meet You

Intermediate
with Guitar Chords

Traditional Irish

© Arranged and Edited by Carrie L. Stuckert 2005

MacPherson's Farewell

Beginner Fingerings

Arranged Carrie L. Stuckert

MacPherson's Farewell

Intermediate
with Guitar Chords

Traditional Scottish

Wild Mountain Thyme

Beginner Fingerings

Traditional Scottish

Note: The second finger on the E string should
be placed between the 1st and 2nd markers.
(1st and 2nd fingers touch)

© Arranged and Edited by Carrie L. Stuckert 2005

Wild Mountain Thyme

Intermediate
with Guitar Chords

Traditional Scottish

23

Erin's Green Shore

Beginner Fingerings

Traditional Irish

Note: The second finger on the E string should
be placed between the 1st and 2nd markers.
(1st and 2nd fingers touch)

© Arranged and Edited by Carrie L. Stuckert 2005

Erin's Green Shore

Intermediate
with Guitar Chords

Traditional Irish

The Salley Gardens

Beginner Fingerings

Traditional Irish

The Salley Gardens

Intermediate
with Guitar Chords

Traditional Irish

After the Battle of Aughrim

Beginner Fingerings

Traditional Irish

Note: The second finger on the E string should be placed between the 1st and 2nd markers. (1st and 2nd fingers touch)

© Arranged and Edited by Carrie L. Stuckert 2005

After the Battle of Aughrim

Intermediate
with Guitar Chords

Traditional Irish

© Arranged and Edited by Carrie L. Stuckert 2005

Bonaparte

Beginner Fingerings

Traditional Irish

Note: The second finger on the A and E strings should
be placed between the 1st and 2nd markers.
(1st and 2nd fingers touch)
Watch for marked accidentals or changes in the music.

© Arranged and Edited by Carrie L. Stuckert 2005

Bonaparte

Intermediate
with Guitar Chords

Traditional Irish

© Arranged and Edited by Carrie L. Stuckert 2005

Star of the County Down

Beginner Fingerings

Traditional Irish

Note: The second finger on the A string should be placed between the 1st and 2nd markers. (1st and 2nd fingers touch)

© Arranged and Edited by Carrie L. Stuckert 2005

Star of the County Down

Intermediate
with Guitar Chords

Traditional Irish

© Arranged and Edited by Carrie L. Stuckert 2005

Itchy Fingers

Beginner Fingerings

Scottish Pipe Tune

Itchy Fingers

Intermediate
with Guitar Chords

Scottish Pipe Tune

© Arranged and Edited by Carrie L. Stuckert 2005

Londonderry Air or Danny Boy

Beginner Fingerings

Traditional Irish

Note: The second finger on the D, A, and E strings should
be placed between the 1st and 2nd markers.
(1st and 2nd fingers touch)
The first finger on the A string should
be placed before the first marker.

© Arranged and Edited by Carrie L. Stuckert 2005

Londonderry Air or Danny Boy

Intermediate
with Guitar Chords

Traditional Irish

© Arranged and Edited by Carrie L. Stuckert 2005

Ballydesmond Polka Set

Beginner Fingerings

Traditional Irish

Violin

Note: The second finger on the A and E strings should
be placed between the 1st and 2nd markers.
(1st and 2nd fingers touch)

First part: The first finger on the E string should
be placed below the 1st marker. The second part
after the key change in measure #18, the first finger should
be placed on the 1st marker.

Ballydesmond Polka Set

Intermediate
with Guitar Chords

Traditional Irish

© Arranged and Edited by Carrie L. Stuckert 2005

Swallow Tail's Jig

Beginner Fingerings

Traditional Irish

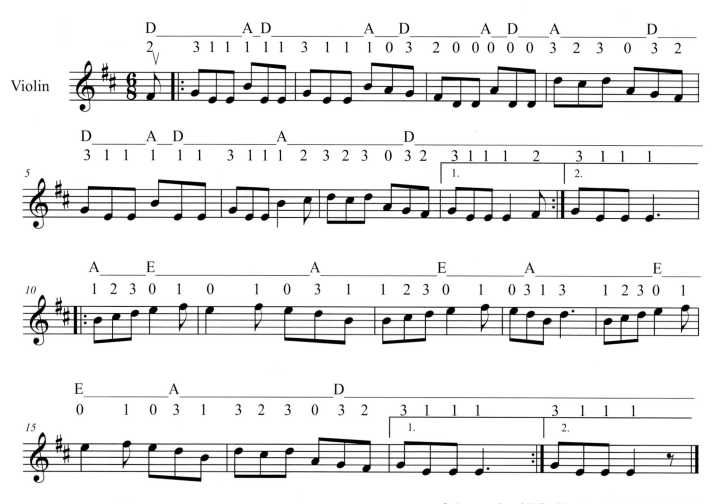

© Arranged and Edited by Carrie L. Stuckert 2005

Swallow Tail's Jig

Intermediate
with Guitar Chords

Traditional Irish

The Irish Washerwoman

Beginner Fingerings

Traditional Irish

Note: The second finger on the A and E strings should
be placed between the 1st and 2nd markers.
(1st and 2nd fingers touch)

© Arranged and Edited by Carrie L. Stuckert 2005

The Irish Washerwoman

Intermediate
with Guitar Chords

Traditional Irish

The Morning Dew

Beginner Fingerings

Traditional Irish

Note: The second finger on the E string should be placed between the 1st and 2nd markers. (1st and 2nd fingers touch)

© Arranged and Edited by Carrie L. Stuckert 2005

The Morning Dew

Intermediate
with Guitar Chords

Traditional Irish

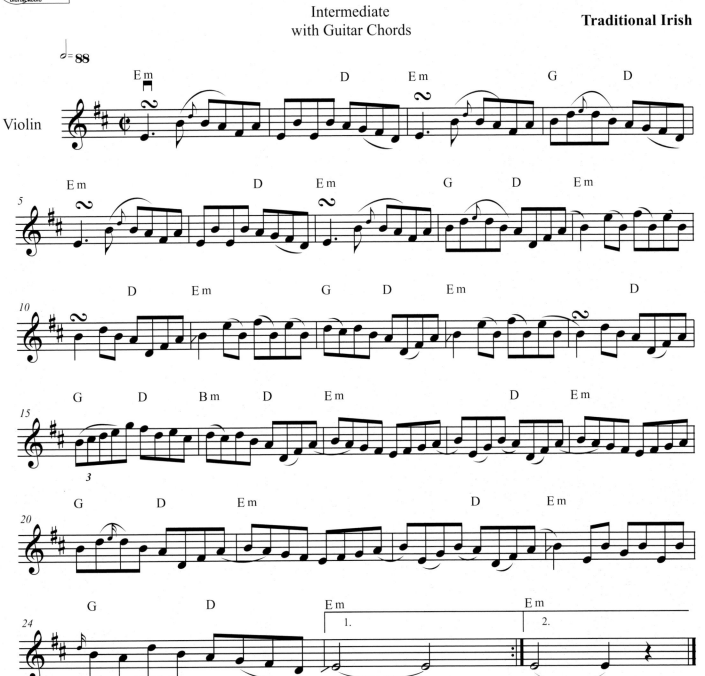

© Arranged and Edited by Carrie L. Stuckert 2005

Banish Misfortune

Beginner Fingerings

Traditional Irish

Note: The second finger on the E string should
be placed between the 1st and 2nd markers.
(1st and 2nd fingers touch)
Watch for accidentals!

© Arranged and Edited by Carrie L. Stuckert 2005

Banish Misfortune

Intermediate
with Guitar Chords

 TRACK 21

Traditional Irish

© Arranged and Edited by Carrie L. Stuckert 2005

About the Author

Carrie Stuckert is an active musician who plays a variety of styles of music spanning from classical, bluegrass, and Celtic to classic rock. She has studied the violin for 27 years and continues to perform and record world-wide. Carrie has taught violin/fiddle lessons for 15 years and through the process of teaching and studying, she developed a Fiddle Tablature to help students learn to play the violin. She has used this method with beginner students for years and it has been incredibly successful. Many students will be playing within hours due to this form of Fiddle Tablature. This method will be available in her book Celtic Fiddling Made Easy through Mel Bay Publications. Carrie has a Master's degree in Education and looks forward to many years of teaching. She continues to teach, perform and record in the Western United States.